Read & Resp

C000022565

CRBURG PRIMARY SCHOOL
CRBURG ROAD
CAMBERWELL
LONDON SE5 0JD
TEL: 0171 703 2583
FAX: 0171 708 0756

FOR KS2

Read & Respond

FOR KS2

Author: Huw Thomas

Development Editor: Alex Albrighton

Assistant Editors: Roanne Charles and Margaret Eaton

Series Designer: Anna Oliwa

Designer: Liz Gilbert

Illustrations: Karen Donnelly

Text © 2010 Huw Thomas © 2010 Scholastic Ltd

Designed using Adobe InDesign

Published by Scholastic Ltd.
Book End, Range Road, Witney,
Oxfordshire OX29 0YD
www.scholastic.co.uk

Printed by Bell & Bain

1 2 3 4 5 6 7 8 9   0 1 2 3 4 5 6 7 8 9

British Library Cataloguing-in-Publication Data
A catalogue record for this book is available from
the British Library.

ISBN 978-1407-11344-9

The right of Huw Thomas to be identified as the author of this work has been asserted by him in accordance with the Copyright, Designs and Patents Act 1988.

Extracts from the Primary National Strategy's *Primary Framework for Literacy* (2006) www.standards.dfes.gov.uk/primaryframework © Crown copyright. Reproduced under the terms of the Click Use Licence.

All rights reserved. This book is sold subject to the condition that it shall not, by way of trade or otherwise, be lent, hired out or otherwise circulated without the publisher's prior consent in any form of binding or cover other than that in which it is published and without a similar condition, including this condition, being imposed upon the subsequent purchaser.

No part of this publication may be reproduced, stored in a retrieval system, or transmitted, in any form or by any means, electronic, mechanical, photocopying, recording or otherwise, without the prior permission of the publisher. This book remains copyright, although permission is granted to copy pages where indicated for classroom distribution and use only in the school which has purchased the book, or by the teacher who has purchased the book, and in accordance with the CLA licensing agreement. Photocopying permission is given only for purchasers and not for borrowers of books from any lending service.

Acknowledgements
The publishers gratefully acknowledge permission to reproduce the following copyright material: **Macmillan Children's Books** for the use of extracts from *Journey to the River Sea* by Eva Ibbotson © 2001, Eva Ibbotson (2001, Macmillan). Every effort has been made to trace copyright holders for the works reproduced in this book, and the publishers apologise for any inadvertent omissions.

Journey to the River Sea

About the book

Journey to the River Sea takes us on a journey with the orphaned Maia to her distant relatives, a thousand miles up the Amazon river. They live in a place called Manaus, the legendary capital of the state of Amazonas. It was here, in the 19th century, that rubber planters, who had made a fortune, created a lavish city in the heart of the forest – including the famous historic theatre which features in this story. Eva Ibbotson first heard of this place from a friend and describes the experience as being like 'that little kick inside the head which means that you have found something that is *yours*'.

Journey to the River Sea is a great example of a historical story. The research shines through in this book and we are transported to a whole other place – but one that was very real. Through the details of the story we enter this bizarre outpost of history. One focus for reading is the degree to which children can enter into the nature of that setting – with a particular focus on the way Maia ventures between starchy civilisation and the wilds of the forest. However, more importantly, this novel is an excellent example of a dilemma story – it presents a story in which characters are faced with various dilemmas. Because of this, another real focus for reading should be the way children understand the points of view of different characters.

About the author

Eva Ibbotson was born in Vienna in 1925 and came to England in 1933, just before the Nazis came to power. Her father was a scientist and her mother was a successful writer who, Eva says, had 'this absolute ability to turn anything into a story'. As a child, following the break-up of her parents' marriage, Eva recalls living with various aunts and grandmothers before being sent to boarding school. She ended up in England at Dartington Hall, a progressive and unusual school, where there was a strong emphasis on children's creativity.

It was an insecure childhood and Eva has commented that her books are often populated by children whose parents 'aren't there', leaving them 'displaced and looking for a home as I was'. It's also one of the reasons she gives the children in her stories a happy ending!

Eva has been writing stories since she was seven years old and *Journey to the River Sea* is one of a number of historical travel stories she has penned. She has also written a lot of magical stories – including *The Secret of Platform 13*, set around Platform 13 of Kings Cross station, years before JK Rowling wrote about Harry Potter and Platform 9.

Describing how she writes, Eva says: 'I write at my mother's old desk, looking out on to a leafy street, and I rewrite what I have written again and again until I get the words the way I want them (most of my pages have been through eight drafts or so). It's my belief that one should be in the same place each day, so that if an idea is hovering it knows where to find you.'

Facts and figures

Journey to the River Sea won the Nestlé Children's Book Prize Gold Award, was runner-up for the Whitbread Children's Book of the Year Award and the Guardian Children's Fiction Prize, and was shortlisted for the Carnegie Medal.

Guided reading

Chapters 1 to 4

Before reading, ask the children what they would think if their family had to move to live in the jungles of the Amazon. What would they be excited about? What would their fears be?

Ask the class to read the first chapter of *Journey to the River Sea*. Stop at this point, firstly to secure the scenario that takes us into the story, and also to consider the initial response to the idea of journeying to the Amazon. Can the children find some of the various ways in which the jungle features in this chapter?

As they read Chapters 2 and 3, ask the children to keep track of the way in which the jungle appears, particularly the vibrancy of the market scene. Encourage them to compare these scenes with their own thoughts about life in the Amazon, and the views Maia encountered back in London, in Chapter 1.

Reading Chapters 2, 3 and 4, draw the children's attention to the characters of Miss Minton and the Carters. In both cases, ask the children to keep track of what sort of characters these individuals present and how they respond to them as readers. Focus particularly on the twins and Maia's expectations, as opposed to the reality she encounters. Ask the children how she must feel, encountering the real twins. What do they think Miss Minton makes of them?

Two predictions can be made as the children work through Chapter 4. Firstly, based on evidence to date, what sort of a relationship do the children think Maia will have with the twins? How will this work out?

Secondly, home in on the final scenes of Chapter 4 and the incident with the tickets, asking the children how they think Maia must feel and encouraging them to imagine what she could do in response.

Chapters 5 to 10

Before they begin Chapter 5, ask the children to reflect on Maia's dilemma and ask themselves what she should do. She has the clear, storybook chance of sneaking off to Manaus. Should she?

Would they? What good and ill could come of such a move?

The way characters feel about the jungle becomes one of the underpinning themes of *Journey to the River Sea* and as the children read Chapter 5, they need to reflect on the narrative arc in this chapter. Maia's experience of the jungle changes. Ask: *How does it change, and why? And who might the mystery boy be?* Bear in mind that when we first read this he appears as if we may never see him again.

Once they have discussed this evolving response, ask the children to read as far as Maia's conversation at the opening of Chapter 7. Looking back at Chapter 5, can they understand what she says about the jungle? What do they think Miss Minton means when she says, *People make their own worlds*?

Revisit Chapter 6 and ask the children to look at the actions of Clovis and the twins. How do we feel about these characters as we turn each page of the novel?

Over the course of Chapters 8 and 9 Clovis and Finn come to the fore and take up a key place in the story, resulting in the plan of Chapter 9. As the children read through the text, split the guided reading group into two. Ask one group to skim through the chapters and chart Maia's encounters with Finn, and the other to do the same for Clovis. Then swap the groups and ask them what each boy is looking for from the girl. When Clovis goes to the Carters' house, or when Finn trusts her, what are they hoping will happen?

As they read Chapter 10, ask the children to bring these thoughts together and explain the complex web of relationships that has evolved between the three of them. What does Maia think of Finn, Finn of Maia, Clovis of Finn, Finn of Clovis and so on?

Chapters 11 to 15

Invite the children to read Chapter 11 and reflect on the way everyone is working to save Finn. What is it that leaves the crows feeling so beaten?

Guided reading

The next few chapters need to be read, then guided. The plot and its hatching make up a core of excitement in the centre of the book. Before they read, ask the children to recall what the plot entails and what the various players will have to do to make it work. How might the other characters be duped or respond as it progresses?

As they read Chapters 12 and 13, see if the children can keep track of the way various characters are being taken in. Is this a good thing? Is it wrong? They may want to discuss the whole business of lying and cheating in a good cause.

Encourage the children to talk about all the bits of the plot and how each one works. What goes smoothly? Where is there a hitch? Home in on that final scene in Chapter 13, the impression being given and what the crows think has happened.

Bearing in mind the deception taking place, ask the children to read Chapters 14 and 15. Focus on the latter chapter. Here we have other characters being duped. Ask: *Is it right that Sir Aubrey should be deceived like this? What could happen to him and Clovis as the story progresses?*

Returning to Chapter 14, ask the children to follow the parallel lines of Maia and Finn, looking at what each one does and feels in response to the other. Focus particularly on their parting, how they each behave, and what we know or think they feel.

Chapters 16 to 20

Ask the children to read Chapters 16 to 18, watching at first for the twins. In a well-told story, we are drawn into the ups and downs of characters, and we do like to see nasty characters get their comeuppance. What is happening to these girls over the course of the chapters? Ask the children to plot the progress of their misery, finding parts of the text that show the journey the girls are taking. Are there things about Mr Carter, in Chapter 18, that remind them of his daughters? What is Miss Minton doing in the face of this misery?

Re-read the final moments of Chapter 18 and check what Mr Carter actually does when there is a fire. What had he said back in Chapter 4?

Once the children have discussed this, ask them to read Chapter 19. Why do the events at the end of Chapter 18 make this such a painful read? What has happened to Maia?

Before they read Chapter 20, ask the children to skim across Chapter 16 again and watch how Finn is changing. What do they think is going on? As they read Chapter 20 there's good news, and a blissful scene of happiness in the jungle. Ask the children to find the two or three sentences that most make this sound as wonderful as it does.

Contrast this chapter with the Carters and their attitude to the jungle in Chapter 3.

Return to Chapter 17 and look at the encounters Clovis is having. He sees his foster mother, but underneath it all there is something he feels he has to do. What do the children think happened at the end of Chapter 17?

Chapters 21 to 24

Chapter 21 is a beautifully written, magical encounter. Ask the children to read it, imagining what Maia and Miss Minton see and hear, and what they think as a result. Can they find two of the most important moments of seeing and hearing in this chapter?

Encourage the children to skim back through other chapters of the book and think about how they have come to know and like the character of Miss Minton. They could compile a list of their 'Top Five Minty Moments' – the five best things she has said and done. The final scene of Chapter 21 is an important moment. Why is this?

Ask the children to read Chapters 22 and 23. Looking from the start of Chapter 21 to the end of Chapter 23, ask the children to think of highs and lows, good and bad things that have happened to Maia and Finn. When have things been good? What makes them turn bad? As these chapters end it's all going badly wrong. What must Finn do and what might happen as a result?

Guided reading

As they read Chapter 24, ask the children to consider how the people's minds change in these pages. What words are said to change their minds and what are people arguing for? Reading the exchange between Miss Minton and Mr Murray, what does each character want for the children? What does Miss Minton mean when she says, *Children must lead big lives*?

With that in mind, as they finish the book invite the children to reflect on what it must be like to be Finn or Maia, and to think about the way different characters have interacted. Choose any two characters and ask what, for example, Clovis thought of Maia (and vice versa).

Shared reading

Extract 1

● Ask the children to imagine they were being sent to live with two children their own age. What sorts of questions would they want to ask?

● Read through the passage, asking the children to pick out all the different things Maia will see on this leg of her journey. How does she feel about what she sees? She could have been scared or sad, but she's actually excited. Why?

● Highlight the words *and didn't stop till they were out of sight*. Encourage the children to look at this section and other clues in the chapter that tell us what sort of person Maia is. What do they imagine she may be like as a friend?

● What do the children think of when they hear the word *free*? Home in on the contrast between captive and free. What does the phrase *Maia was free to make up their lives* mean?

● Why do the children think the twins had written such a short letter to Maia? It leaves her free to imagine their lives. Is this a good thing? Would it have been better to know more about them?

Extract 2

● Read this passage after Maia's first journey into the jungle in Chapter 5. Display the first half of the passage, as far as the words *What I thought was there*.

● Invite the children to read the passage, as far as the hidden section, asking themselves what it tells us about the relationship between Miss Minton and Maia and what each of them is thinking.

● Ask the children to pick out the change that has come across Maia, seen clearly in this shared text. What has changed and why? Highlight the words *I've seen that it is there*. What is the *it* that Maia thought was out there?

● Now display the rest of the passage to the class. Look at the way the section beginning *I mean... the forest...* is written. Ask the children why is it written in that way. Invite one or two children to read this paragraph aloud in the tone and manner in which they think Maia said it. Encourage the children to think of stories they have written where, once in the story, a character could talk in this way.

● Look at Miss Minton's final line. What does she mean by this?

Extract 3

● Invite the children to read the passage in this extract and consider what we are told about Miss Minton. What sort of impression does this build up? (Someone who won't chase a butterfly and who tries not to feel excited.) The children may like to add their thoughts from other parts of the story.

● Read the moment when Miss Minton sees and clambers towards the butterfly, and contrast it with the person who won't chase or get excited. What has happened to her and why?

● Read the moment where Miss Minton takes the dead butterfly, and ask the children to describe how it would feel to do this.

● Highlight the words *even Furo shook his head* and ask why these words are special. What does this tell us about the find?

● Invite the children to consider Miss Minton's final words on the find – why does she say this? Tease out the way she doesn't want to raise expectations but then ask why, this being the case, she keeps looking at the creature in her lap.

Extract 1

Chapter 2

They passed plantations of rubber trees and Indian villages with the houses built on stilts to stop them being flooded when the river rose. The Indian children came out onto the landing stage and waved and called out, and Maia waved back and didn't stop till they were out of sight.

Sometimes the boat went close enough to the shore for them to pass by old houses owned by the sugar planters or coffee exporters; they could see the verandas with the families taking tea, and dogs stretched out in the shade, and hanging baskets of scarlet flowers.

'Will it be like that?' Maia kept asking. 'They're sure to have a veranda, aren't they – perhaps we can do lessons looking out over the river?'

She was becoming more and more excited. The colour, the friendly waving Indians, the flashing birds, all delighted her, and she was not troubled by the heat. But at the centre of all her thoughts were the twins. She saw them in white dresses with coloured sashes like pictures in a book, laughing and welcoming and friendly. She imagined them getting ready for bed, brushing each other's hair, and lying in a hammock with a basket full of kittens on their laps, or picking flowers for the house.

'They'll have a big garden going down to the river, don't you think?' she asked Miss Minton, 'and a boat with a striped awning probably. I don't really like fishing because of the hooks but if they showed me… I suppose you can live off the land in a place like that.'

Since the letter the twins had written to her was only two sentences long, Maia was free to make up their lives, and she did this endlessly.

Text © 2001, Eva Ibbotson.

SCHOLASTIC
www.scholastic.co.uk

Extract 2

Chapter 7

In the evening, when Miss Minton came to 'hear her read', Maia said, 'I'm not staying here without you. I shall write to Mr Murray.'

'I think you will find that at the salary the Carters are paying me, it might take a little while to find someone else,' said Miss Minton dryly. She picked up Maia's hairbrush. 'Don't tell me you're doing a hundred strokes a night because I don't believe it. I've told you again and again that you must look after your hair.' She picked up the brush and brushed fiercely for a while. And then: 'Do you want to go back, Maia? Back to England?'

'I did,' she said, thinking about it. 'The twins are so awful and there seemed no point in being here, shut up in this house. But not now. I don't want to go now because I've seen that it is there. What I thought was there.'

Miss Minton waited.

'I mean … the forest … the river … the Amazon … everything I thought of before I came. And the people who live in it and know about it.'

Then she told Miss Minton about the boy who had taken her into Manaus.

'He didn't speak English, but he had such a listening face; I couldn't believe he didn't understand everything I said. Oh, Minty, it was such a wonderful journey, like floating through a drowned forest. You can't believe it's the same world as the Carters live in.'

'It isn't,' said Miss Minton. 'People make their own worlds.'

Text © 2001, Eva Ibbotson; illustration © 2010, Karen Donnelly.

Extract 3

Chapter 14

It was as they came away from the lagoon in Furo's canoe that Miss Minton suddenly told Furo to stop. A breeze had sprung up and as the leaves of a tall broad-leafed tree blew to one side, she had seen on its trunk, a large and most exquisite butterfly.

Miss Minton did not chase butterflies, but this one was so enormous and so beautiful – and so still – that she clambered out of the canoe and went to look.

'My goodness!' she said.

The butterfly was still because it was dead. Dead, but perfectly preserved in the web of a large spider who had left it there, and would probably come back and eat it later.

Very carefully, Miss Minton took the butterfly from the tree, using her handkerchief so as not to touch it directly, and carried it back.

'Oh!' said Maia. 'I've never seen anything like that!', and even Furo shook his head.

The brilliant yellow and black of the wings ended in two long tails, like the tail of a swallow.

'It looks special, doesn't it?' Maia went on. 'Professor Glastonberry will know what it is.'

Miss Minton nodded, trying not to feel excited. 'It is most unlikely that it will turn out to be anything unusual,' she said firmly, but Maia saw her looking at the creature lying on her lap again and again.

PHOTOCOPIABLE

Text © 2001, Eva Ibbotson; illustration © 2010, Karen Donnelly.

SCHOLASTIC
www.scholastic.co.uk

READ & RESPOND: Activities based on *Journey to the River Sea*

Plot, character and setting

Meeting Miss Minton

> **Objective:** To understand underlying themes, causes and points of view.
> **What you need:** Copies of *Journey to the River Sea*, flipchart paper and pens.

What to do

● Ask the children to recall their first encounters with a new teacher at school. What impression did they form and what built up that picture? You could share a childhood example.

● Draw out the effects of a person's appearance, their actions, the things they say, and the things others say about them. Make a central list of these for children to refer to as they do the next steps.

● Reading the closing pages of Chapter 1, ask the children to take a good look at this first meeting with Miss Minton, keeping an eye on the features mentioned earlier.

● Working in groups, encourage the children to present their impressions of Miss Minton by making notes in whatever form they choose on a piece of flipchart paper. The more scattered their notes the better, as more will be added.

● Direct the children to five aspects of this introduction – the other children's comments, the skeletal gloved hand, the comments about friendship, the hatpin and Henry Hartington.

● Once the children have completed their notes they can compare ideas. These should then be kept and added to as the story progresses – with children being allowed to volunteer when a comment or action (such as the later theft and corsetry) causes them to add to their notes.

> **Differentiation**
> **For older/more confident learners:** Encourage the children to consider how the reader's impression of Miss Minton grows, page by page.
> **For younger/less confident learners:** Ask the children to focus on one aspect of the character – appearance is a good one to choose.

The market and the bungalow

> **Objective:** To understand underlying themes, causes and points of view.
> **What you need:** Copies of *Journey to the River Sea* and copies of photocopiable page 15.

What to do

● Ask the children to think about a memorable story setting that they can picture in their mind and the things that help them to imagine they are there, with the characters.

● Now read aloud the descriptions of the market and the Carters' bungalow from the end of Chapter 2 and the start of Chapter 3. Don't ask the children to read along with you, but encourage them to picture the two settings as they listen.

● Give each child a copy of photocopiable page 15 to complete without looking at the text. They should use their own memories of the pictures that formed in their heads as you read. Encourage them to try to imagine what each place is like from Maia's point of view.

● Once they have made their own notes, invite the children to work with a partner, comparing their thoughts and catching things they missed out. You could mention the use of colours, or that one setting mentions a clear smell, whereas another leaves it to the imagination.

● Re-read the passages with the children and check any other details worth noting. They can annotate their sheet with additional thoughts.

> **Differentiation**
> **For older/more confident learners:** Invite them to try imagining other features of the setting.
> **For younger/less confident learners:** Help the children to work through the text and explore the aspects of setting on photocopiable page 15. Make notes of their comments and observations on the grid.

Plot, character and setting

Questions and answers

Objective: To make notes and use evidence from across a text to explain events or ideas.
What you need: Copies of *Journey to the River Sea* and copies of photocopiable page 16.

What to do
- Before they begin reading Chapter 3, ask the children to think about the previous two chapters and to list any questions they have so far in their reading of *Journey to the River Sea*. These could be about why things have occurred – for example, *Why are the Carters taking in Maia?* – or about things yet to occur – such as, *What will it be like at the Carters' home?*
- Ask the children to look through photocopiable page 16 and read the list of questions they will encounter as they read. They should stop as they reach each question and record their own thoughts about what the answer could

be, in the space indicated.
- Encourage the children to share their answers with others, making the point that more variety is a good thing in a task like this. For example, if they all conclude the whistler is the maid, it's not as much fun as imagining how it could be Mr Carter, or one of the twins, who lives a secret life in the compound.
- Before they reach the end of Chapter 3, the children will already have the answers to some of their questions. They can start filling in the 'The answer' boxes and solve the mysteries as they read the rest of the book.

Differentiation
For older/more confident learners: Children can keep a log of similar questions and answers as they read further into the story.
For younger/less confident learners: Present the children with a limited number of questions.

Minor characters

Objective: To explore how writers use language for comic and dramatic effects.
What you need: Copies of *Journey to the River Sea*.

What to do
- Challenge the children to list every single character they can think of in *Journey to the River Sea*. By the third page in the book we have already met nine, so their list should be extensive.
- Working in small groups, ask the children to isolate a list of five characters who only appear in a few pages across the novel – so, for example, Clovis's families are fine, but not the boy himself. The children's task is to piece together memorable features of these folks, even though they rarely appear in the book.
- Give a lead by mentioning Miss Emily (from Maia's London school) or the police chief who works so hard at hiding Finn. You could

also point the children towards some of the memorable things these characters say, even though they make only a brief walk through the story. Good examples include Mr Haltmann's beautiful words about Brazil in Chapter 11 or the countess's words of welcome in Chapter 12.
- Encourage the children to make notes about their characters and then feed back to a whole-class discussion.

Differentiation
For older/more confident learners: Children could set themselves the challenge of increasing their inventory of minor characters, considering what they each bring to the story.
For younger/less confident learners: Give the children a particular character to work on and specific pages to explore. The countess is a good choice – particularly as the elegant woman is described as *untidy*.

Plot, character and setting

Misdirection

Objective: To deduce characters' reasons for behaviour from their actions.
What you need: Copies of *Journey to the River Sea* and copies of photocopiable page 17.

What to do

● Ask the children to re-read Chapters 12 and 13, paying particular attention to the plot that Finn had hatched and the role Maia and Clovis play in it. They should also note how the twins and crows feature in this turn in the plotline.

● Encourage the children to pick out the various points at which a character does something that is part of the plan and how it affects others around them, paying particular attention to how the 'trick' is being played. Ask: *How does it look to them? How are they being misled?*

● Once they have re-read the chapters, ask the children to look at photocopiable page 17.

● Working in pairs, encourage the children to imagine they are the twins, and then that they are the crows. After each of the moments listed, what do they think these characters could have said to each other? How would they explain what had just happened?

● Working individually, ask the children to complete the photocopiable sheet. Note that the questions pick up on particular aspects of how characters would respond to a repeated behaviour or the words a character spoke.

Differentiation
For older/more confident learners: Ask the children to root out some of the other characters and consider the role they play in the deception or how it appears to them – particular mention is made of Sergei and Miss Minton, who have differing responses.
For younger/less confident learners: Children could read one of the pieces of misdirection and imagine it from the twins' point of view.

Point of view

Objective: To infer writers' perspectives from what is written and from what is implied.
What you need: Copies of *Journey to the River Sea* and lots of bits of paper cut into cloud shapes.

What to do

● Show the children the famous *Guardian* advert. It is available on the internet and can be accessed by entering 'Guardian Advert Point of View' into a search engine. Point out that there can be a multitude of perspectives on events.

● Ask the children to re-read the following three episodes in the story and ask themselves how each would have looked to the character concerned: Maia's 'attack' in the boat at the end of Chapter 5, Finn picking over the wreckage in Chapter 20 and Captain Pereia's perception of songs and corsets in Chapter 23.

● Invite the children to work in groups of three.

They should write headings in the thought-bubble clouds and then record how these situations will have appeared to, and been perceived by, these characters at the time. What would they have thought about them?

● Once they have done this, ask the children to gather their thoughts (literally) about each episode and read through them. They can then read the successive paragraphs where the characters discover what was actually going on, and compare the two versions.

Differentiation
For older/more confident learners: Invite the children to put together a monologue of Captain Pereia's recount of his experiences in Chapter 23.
For younger/less confident learners: Support children in this activity by just looking at the episode with Maia in the boat.

Plot, character and setting

Cliffhanging

> **Objective:** To compare the usefulness of techniques such as prediction in exploring the meaning of texts.
> **What you need:** Copies of *Journey to the River Sea*, sheets of A3 paper and pens.

What to do

● Ask the children to come up with some examples of cliffhanger endings from recent viewing of soaps, dramas or action on the television. Home in on the difference between ones that underline the preceding actions and ones that change it. In the latter endings there can be a sudden twist (such as the entrance of a character we thought was dead, and the title music pounds in). In the former, something is said or done that emphasises the fact that all is not well – such as a character issuing an ultimatum – and we will want to know how things will be resolved.

● Working in groups of five or six, ask the children to read the endings of Chapters 15 to 20, focusing on the final two or three lines in each instance.

● Encourage the children to write down what they think are the key words or phrases in the centre of a large sheet of paper and then write around these words some of the questions or clues that such words will put into the reader's mind as to what might follow.

> **Differentiation**
> **For older/more confident learners:** Encourage the children to review the types of cliffhanger noted above and reflect on which of these jobs the examples they have analysed are doing.
> **For younger/less confident learners:** Children can focus on two or three consecutive chapter endings, reflecting on the chapter that precedes them and the significance of the ending.

Why did they say that?

> **Objective:** To explore how writers use language for comic and dramatic effects.
> **What you need:** Copies of *Journey to the River Sea* and copies of photocopiable page 18.

What to do

● Begin by looking at the first quote on photocopiable page 18. Ask the children if they can recall who said it, and when. They may even be able to locate the quote in the book or have some idea of what preceded and followed it.

● Together with the class, re-read the end of Chapter 20 and look at the quote on the photocopiable sheet as it appears in the book. Invite the children to think of why those words matter, not just in the moment in which they were said. (The words say something about the whole story – about Finn's life and Maia's wish to join it.)

● Now distribute copies of photocopiable page

18 and explain that the other quotes all come from Chapters 21 or 22. Tell the children that they will need to read the quotes and work out where each one could have appeared in the story. They can then make notes on why each quote was said.

● Remind the children to consider each quote in relation to the story as a whole – for example, a dropped corset in itself isn't as significant as one in a story where it has been a symbol of the constraints imposed on a character!

> **Differentiation**
> **For older/more confident learners:** Ask the children to locate their own lines like these ones in later chapters, highlighting ones that have greater significance for the story as a whole.
> **For younger/less confident learners:** Cut up photocopiable page 18 and focus the children on a limited number of quotes.

SECTION
4

The market and the bungalow

● Listen to your teacher reading the descriptions of the market scene and the Carters' bungalow in Chapters 2 and 3 of *Journey to the River Sea*. Think about the pictures that appear in your head and try to imagine them from Maia's point of view. Make some brief notes on this sheet.

	The market	The bungalow
What would Maia see?		
What sounds would she hear?		
What would it smell like?		
What would other people be doing?		
What would it feel like?		

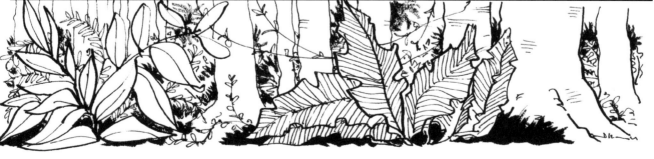

Illustration © 2010, Karen Donnelly.

SECTION
4

Questions and answers

● Read these questions and write down what you think the answers are.
As you encounter each one in the book, you can note what the real answer
turned out to be.

But Maia lingered for a moment, looking down at the palm of her outstretched hand.
What was odd about the handshake?

I think

The answer

But just before she left the window she heard somebody whistling.
Who mysteriously whistles 'Blow the Wind Southerly'?

I think

The answer

Miss Minton … knew exactly why they had offered to have Maia.
Why have the Carters really offered to take Maia?

I think

The answer

But when Miss Minton asked Maia to read a paragraph, she stopped her almost at once.
Why isn't Maia allowed to read?

I think

The answer

Misdirection

● In Chapters 12 and 13 of *Journey to the River Sea*, Maia, Finn and Clovis enact their big deception. Looking at these moments from the plot, work out how they looked to others in the story and what was really happening:

Maia looks out of the big window three times.

Why would the twins
imagine she keeps looking?

Maia's prayer.

What would the twins
think she means?

The sandwich and the nuts.

What would the twins
think these are for?

Maia's pleading: 'You don't want him to be caught…'

How would that sound
to the twins?

Clovis says: 'Unhand my servant.'

What would the crows
think is going on?

Clovis gives the watch to Finn.

What would the crows
make of this?

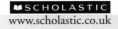

Plot, character and setting

Why did they say that?

● As *Journey to the River Sea* moves to its conclusion, the action heats up and everyone has a lot to say.

● Find these lines in the story and explain what is going on.

> We've got all the time in the world.

_____

_____

> Oh no! Not the Carters!

_____

_____

> We shall have to steal one.

_____

_____

> When we're grown up I'll come back for you, I promise.

_____

_____

> If you *must* know… it was my corset.

_____

_____

> It may be awful here, but at least we won't get eaten.

_____

_____

PHOTOCOPIABLE

SCHOLASTIC
www.scholastic.co.uk

READ & RESPOND: Activities based on *Journey to the River Sea*

Talk about it

Talklines

> **Objective:** To explore how writers use language for comic and dramatic effects.
> **What you need:** Copies of *Journey to the River Sea*, copies of photocopiable page 22, flipchart paper and pens.

What to do
● Ask the class if they can recall one-liners that were really important in stories or films they know. For a certain generation, 'May the force be with you' is a resonant example. They may be able to recall catchphrases from recent films.
● In groups of four or six, ask the children to skim through Chapters 1 to 3. As they do so, they should discuss among their group any sentences that stand out for their beauty or importance.
● Now give the groups a limited time to discuss the sentences on photocopiable page 22. Cut these up and explain to the children that their larger group needs to split into sub-groups to discuss these words and note down thoughts to share with the wider group.
● Explain to the children they could look at what the sentence is about, why such words would be said and what they make the reader think about events or characters in the story.

> **Differentiation**
> **For older/more confident learners:** Encourage the children to rank the lines according to which they think was the most memorable and to explain why.
> **For younger/less confident learners:** The activity can be done purely as a locating exercise. Ask the children to find these words in the book by recalling the story and matching the language.

Expecting twins

> **Objective:** To recognise rhetorical devices used to mislead and sway the reader.
> **What you need:** Copies of *Journey to the River Sea*.

What to do
● Invite the children to talk about times when they are going to meet up with relatives they haven't seen for a long time. Do they look forward to it? Do they get on well? How do they feel as the minutes tick by?
● Ask the children to re-read the second half of Chapter 2, looking at the way Maia builds up her hopes regarding the twins and their lives. Ask: *What sort of life does she envisage? How does she feel about this? In particular, what image does she have of the twins and their home?* Note, also, what she does at the market. Encourage the children to discuss this with their partners.
● In their pairs, invite the children to read Chapter 3 up to the part where Maia goes to sleep on her first day, and to discuss what she would be thinking as she lay there that night. If it helps, they can imagine they are her, talking aloud about how the day has gone. The main focus should be on whether the twins have met her expectations and what she feels about this.
● Ask the children to predict how Maia's relationship with the twins could develop. They should think about Maia, Miss Minton, the twins and their parents, and also the facts that Clovis is in Manaus and there is an incredible jungle just outside the bungalow.
● Ask the children to 'twin up' with their partners again after they have read some more moments involving Beatrice and Gwendolyn.

> **Differentiation**
> **For older/more confident learners:** Ask the children to re-read other passages that contain the twins and make notes on these characters.
> **For younger/less confident learners:** This activity can be moved from being a comparison of expectations and actuality to just a consideration of what the twins are like, with particular reflection on how they treat Maia in Chapters 3 and 4.

Talk about it

Minty and Prof

Objective: To sustain engagement with longer texts, using different techniques to make texts come alive.
What you need: Copies of *Journey to the River Sea*.
Cross-curricular link: PSHE.

What to do

● Ask the children to think of interesting relationships in stories they know. This may include some quirky romances from comedies or soaps. Ask them why they enjoy watching characters like these as they spark off each other.
● In groups of four to six, encourage the children to read Chapter 10 to themselves. Still working independently, they need to make notes on what sort of relationship these two characters have.
● To engender some responses, invite the children to consider things from each character's point of view. Ask: *What is the Professor thinking about Minty and what is she thinking about him?*

● Once they have made their notes, invite the children to share them with their groups. They should also aim to find lines of text and moments in the chapter that support all their thoughts. So, for example, if one child says: *I think he respects her*, it becomes the whole group's task to find text that would support this suggestion.
● Ask the children predict the future for these two characters. The fact is, when the book ends we don't know what will come of their relationship.

Differentiation
For older/more confident learners: Invite the children to come up with two possibilities for how the relationship between Minty and the Professor will progress after the story.
For younger/less confident learners: Ask the children to reflect on the relationship and make notes on their thoughts, without the hunt through the text for supporting information.

Say it with feeling

Objective: To perform a scripted scene making use of dramatic conventions.
What you need: Copies of *Journey to the River Sea* and copies of photocopiable page 23.

What to do

● Set the children to work in pairs (preferably a boy and a girl). Ask these pairs to read the opening conversation between Maia and Finn in Chapter 11, looking at how it connects with everything that has gone before and discussing the stage they are at in their friendship. Once they have read the conversation they need to consider what tone the different lines have.
● Give each child a copy of photocopiable page 23 and ask them to read the conversation, with one child reading Finn's words and the other reading Maia's.
● Explain to the children that they should now re-read the script and annotate it with directions

they would give actors if they were telling them how to act the scene for a film of *Journey to the River Sea*. They can insert directions as to the way things are to be said, including words such as *Angry* or phrases such as *Realising what she has just said*. Remind the children that they need to consider again what the motives are of the characters as they say each line and inject that mood into the dialogue.
● As the children work, check that they have read the direction already written in the book – such as Finn's frown, or the way he is not pleased at something Maia says.

Differentiation
For older/more confident learners: Children with a talent for drama may be able to memorise and act out this section of the story.
For younger/less confident learners: Encourage the children to read the script and then combine it with their own *ad lib* to create the scene.

Talk about it

Attitudes to the jungle

Objective: To use the techniques of dialogic talk to explore ideas, topics or issues.
What you need: Copies of *Journey to the River Sea* and copies of photocopiable page 24.
Cross-curricular link: Geography.

What to do

● Ask the children what they think of when they hear the word *jungle* and to explain their responses. If, for example, someone says *exciting*, follow up what it is about this environment we think would induce that response. Encourage the children to think of different characters in *Journey to the River Sea* and the ways they react to the prospect of being in the jungle.
● Hand out copies of photocopiable page 24. Working in groups of four, ask the children to read through it. Tell them not to fill in the sheet until the end – the main focus is discussion.

● As they consider the responses, encourage the children to find not just each character's attitude, but something of what they say that explains why they feel the way they do.
● Invite the children to share their views within their groups, and then to complete the photocopiable sheet.
● Finish by asking the children to respond as a group to the characters' attitudes, trying as far as they can to see where they can empathise and understand and also where they differ from the thinking of these characters.

Differentiation
For older/more confident learners: Challenge the children to look elsewhere in the book, such as Chapters 20 and 23, exploring further developments in characters' attitudes towards the jungle.
For younger/less confident learners: Children could consider one or two sections on the sheet.

Families

Objective: To use the techniques of dialogic talk to explore ideas, topics or issues.
What you need: Copies of *Journey to the River Sea*, slips of paper and writing materials.
Cross-curricular link: PSHE.

What to do

● When the children have finished the story, read 'About the author' on page 3 of this book, asking the children to listen out for ways in which Eva Ibbotson's experience may be seen in the way she writes about Maia. Note what she says about childhood and insecurity. Ask: *How is this reflected in the character of Maia?*
● Discuss with the children their own families, friends and neighbours. Ask: *What support do these people give? Can families sometimes be difficult?*
● On slips of paper, write the names of the children in *Journey to the River Sea*. Ask the class to select one of these characters and to share with

a partner their thoughts on the sort of family support that the character has. You may want to prompt them to consider the role the Professor plays in Finn's life, the way the twins relate to their father, the way Maia doesn't make it to the bosom of her new family and the way Clovis is treated by the Goodleys.
● Then discuss as a class the sorts of families the children in *Journey to the River Sea* have around them and the way they relate to them. Ask: *Do these relationships have things in common? What are the biggest differences?*

Differentiation
For older/more confident learners: Children can create a chart in which they can make notes about the way the children relate to their families, drawing links between any similarities and noting differences.
For younger/less confident learners: Direct the children towards Clovis and the issues in his relationships, particularly with the Goodleys.

Talk about it

Talklines

● Cut out these lines from *Journey to the River Sea* and share them with your group. Talk about what each line tells you and what it makes you think.

'For whether a place is a hell or a heaven rests in yourself, and those who go with courage and an open mind may find themselves in Paradise.'

The Goodleys were not exactly nasty, but they behaved as if no one existed in the world except themselves.

It seemed to her really sad that a boy should have to worry about getting spots – and that he shouldn't be at all excited about travelling to the Amazon.

Since the letter the twins had written to her was only two sentences long, Maia was free to make up their lives, and she did this endlessly.

It looked as though the Carters were pretending they were still in England.

PHOTOCOPIABLE

www.scholastic.co.uk

READ RESPOND: Activities based on *Journey to the River Sea*

Talk about it

SECTION
5

Say it with feeling

● Read this conversation between Maia and Finn, and add directions to describe how the actors should say each line.

Finn	After he's been there a week, he'll be talking like Sir Aubrey or braying like Joan... But he's such a coward.
Maia	I don't think it's cowardly to be afraid of hiding in a dark cellar and waiting to be snatched by two horrible crows.
Finn	You're always defending him.
Maia	Well, he's alone in the world.
Finn	So am I alone in the world.
Maia	No, you aren't. You've got Lila who adores you, and Professor Glastonberry and the chief of police, and all the Indians here. And when you get to the Xanti you'll probably have lots and lots of relatives. Aunts and uncles and cousins – and maybe grandparents too. A huge family...
Finn	Do you think so? I hadn't thought of it like that.
Maia	It's sure to be like that. Whereas Clovis and I don't have anybody.
Finn	You've got Miss Minton… And you've got me.
Maia	But you're going away.
Finn	Yes. That's true. I'm going away.

Attitudes to the jungle

● Look at these chapters of *Journey to the River Sea* and work out what these different characters think about the jungle.

Chapter 1 The girls at Maia's school	**Chapter 3** Mrs Carter
Chapter 5 Maia, on her first visit to the jungle	**Chapter 7** Maia, after her visit to the jungle

Illustration © 2010, Karen Donnelly.

Get writing

The plan

> **Objective:** To use varied structures to shape and organise text coherently.
> **What you need:** Copies of *Journey to the River Sea*, sheets of A3 paper and pens.

What to do
● Working in twos and threes, ask the children to read the final pages of Chapter 9 in which Finn's plan is hatched. They need to check that they understand the plan – who is involved, what they do and how this looks to others.
● Invite the groups to draft on A3 paper a planning document that would plot the various bits of Finn's plan as a way of explaining it to others. One way of bringing this to life would be for the children to imagine that they actually are Finn, faced with the task of explaining the plan to others. What type of chart would they devise?

● Point out that the plan will involve other people, so the children need to ensure that their document shows who is involved and what they will do. Advise them that they will need to show the progression in the plan, perhaps using arrows or numbered steps. They need to show how one thing causes, or is caused by, another.
● As an evaluative stage, groups could swap plans with each other, charging their readers to read the plan as if they were approaching it for the first time. Would it work?

> **Differentiation**
> **For older/more confident learners:** Children could devise their own scheme to save Finn, drawing on the various characters and resources in the book.
> **For younger/less confident learners:** Ask the children to each take a separate section of the plan and work as a group to construct it, by working together and linking their ideas.

Back stories

> **Objective:** To experiment with different narrative forms and styles to write their own stories.
> **What you need:** Copies of *Journey to the River Sea*, photocopiable page 28 and writing materials.

What to do
● Remind the children of the features of explanatory texts, focusing particularly on the 'cause and effect' way in which one thing leads to another. Ask them to think of any examples they have read or to find some examples from their own writing.
● Distribute copies of photocopiable page 28. Discuss the way in which *Journey to the River Sea* draws together a number of stories from the past, all coming to a head in this period of time on the Amazon. Read through the photocopiable sheet and introduce the term 'back story', used to describe the events from the past that a character brings to a story.

● Ask the children to read through the parts of *Journey to the River Sea* and use the prompts to make notes about the events of the back story and the way they caused the situation in the present.
● Once they have made their notes the children can use these as the basis for a writing project. Their task is to imagine that they are Finn, Maia, Miss Minton or the Professor writing a letter to one of the other characters. The letter should explain how the various things that happened in the past all came together in the events of *Journey to the River Sea*, and what might have happened if things had turned out differently.

> **Differentiation**
> **For older/more confident learners:** Challenge the children to write a dialogue featuring two characters in the back story, from that time.
> **For younger/less confident learners:** Ask the children just to pick out and make notes on the three back stories.

Get writing

Becoming someone

Objective: To adapt non-narrative forms and styles to write factual texts.
What you need: Copies of *Journey to the River Sea* and writing materials.

What to do
● Discuss the idea of someone pretending to be someone they aren't. Children may be able to think of examples from stories or films. Using their imaginations, what sorts of things would they need to master to be able to carry off such a stunt? Make notes on the board.
● Ask the children to re-read the opening pages of Chapter 12, where Clovis's deception begins. Encourage them to find some of the things he has to do to pass himself off as Finn. They could also look back to the last pages of Chapter 10 where Clovis has to learn about Westwood.
● Working in groups of four, ask the children to devise a set of instructions for anyone wishing to engage in such a deception. They need to write this as an instructional text, with a 'What you need' section and imperative commands. Looking through these sections of the story, they can draw out some of the things needed to carry off the deception.
● Once the instructions are written, the children could devise imaginative scenarios in which they may need such instructions. For example: *Imagine you had to go to a posh school and pretend you were from another country's royal family.*

Differentiation
For older/more confident learners: Children can take their instructions and read later in the book to evaluate how effectively Clovis carried them out.
For younger/less confident learners: Children can focus on one section of Clovis's life at Westwood and consider how this would challenge him.

Love story

Objective: To use different narrative techniques to engage and entertain the reader.
What you need: Copies of *Journey to the River Sea*, photocopiable page 29 and writing materials.
Cross-curricular link: PSHE.

What to do
● Be honest – *Journey to the River Sea* is, among other things, a love story. Tell the children they are going to explore that strand of the book as the basis for devising their own story of a boy and girl meeting and growing closer. (As a concession to those who are violently opposed to such writing, you could focus more on friendship than romance!)
● Hand out copies of photocopiable page 29 and ask the children to work through it, using it as the basis for a reflection on what two characters think of each other as a story progresses.
● Invite the children to plan their own story of two young people getting to know each other – turning it into a love story if they wish. They should use some of the features of the relationship described in *Journey to the River Sea* – such as the initial non-recognition or the strand of jealousy – as the basis for their own story idea.
● Set the class the task of writing part or all of their stories, but as they do this they can refer both to the book and their results from photocopiable page 29, looking for further insights into the nuances of a relationship. Point out that these often emerge in what two characters say as they talk to each other.

Differentiation
For older/more confident learners: Ask the children to consider how the subtlety of the relationship works. How does it grow over time?
For younger/less confident learners: Encourage the children to work in small groups and each look at one of the strands in Maia and Finn's relationship.

Get writing

Twin notes

> **Objective:** To create multi-layered texts.
> **What you need:** Copies of *Journey to the River Sea*, small sheets of scrap and note paper, and a large sheet of display paper.

What to do
● Ask the children to imagine they won a huge sum of money – what would they do with it? After listing a few dreams, encourage them to think how such a win could change them. Ask: *How might it alter your family life and friendships? Would you share it? Would people expect you to?*
● In groups, ask the children to read Chapters 16, 18 and 22, and look at how the money and other changes come upon the Carters.
● Now, in pairs, ask the children to imagine they are Beatrice and Gwendolyn and that, following the deterioration in their relationship, the two girls increasingly wrote notes to themselves (or others) that they pinned up on doors, left on chairs and pillows, and passed around as a huffy means of communication.
● Skim-reading these chapters again, ask the children to find 12 occasions (six each) when the girls would have written such notes. Their task is to write replicas of the actual notes. These can be done on scrappy, torn bits of paper (like real-life notes) and displayed on a larger sheet in the order in which they were written.
● As an add-on to the activity, the children could write some replies from the parents.

> **Differentiation**
> **For older/more confident learners:** Challenge the children to look at how Mr Carter behaves and to feature this in their notes.
> **For younger/less confident learners:** This activity can be limited to a focus on Chapter 16 where the money really begins to affect the twins.

Maia's scrapbook

> **Objective:** To integrate words, images and sounds imaginatively for different purposes.
> **What you need:** Copies of *Journey to the River Sea*, copies of photocopiable page 30, access to the internet, glue, scissors, drawing materials, watercolour paints and scrapbooks (either made or bought).
> **Cross-curricular link:** Science.

What to do
● Ask the children to imagine Maia's journey up the Amazon and what she would have seen. What would it have been like if she had kept a scrapbook to record the wildlife she encountered?
● Make a class list of the sorts of things she would have put in such a book, including writings, notes, sketches, paintings and so on.
● Ask the children to work in groups of four or five, and hand out copies of photocopiable page 30. Explain that they are going to produce a scrapbook that will include Maia's notes. They can cut up the sheet and share the animals among the group. Their task is to research and create short pieces of written information about these creatures by looking at online encyclopedias.
● Remind the children that they should only include what they think Maia would have recorded. So, for example, if they find ten pages of information they need to choose just the sections that would have interested Maia most.
● The note pages can be embellished by drawings and other items – for example, the children may want to include a watercolour, a paw-print or a black and white photograph.

> **Differentiation**
> **For older/more confident learners:** Ask the children to look for more animals that are mentioned in the book and add these to their scrapbooks – for example, capuchin, gecko, umbrella bird and egret.
> **For younger/less confident learners:** Children can be given a limited number of animals to research.

Back stories

- Using the grid below, explore the back stories of these characters from *Journey to the River Sea*.

	What happened?	What if this hadn't happened?	How does this link to the events in the jungle?	How did it turn out?
Chapter 9: Bernard's story				
Chapter 11: The Carters' story				
Chapter 14: Miss Minton's story				

Love story

● Find these sections of *Journey to the River Sea* and follow the developing love story between Maia and Finn.

Their first meeting: Why was it so strange?

Chapter 11: How do they get on? Look his first words to her.

The end of Chapter 14: Why do they hide what they really feel?

Chapter 16: What is changing for Finn and how do we know it?

Life together in Chapter 20: What's so good about this time?

Conclusion in Chapter 24: What do we learn from Finn's talk with Clovis?

Get writing

SECTION 6

Maia's scrapbook

● Research these animals and write about them in your scrapbook. What other animals do we encounter in the story?

Chapter 2 — fresh water dolphin	Chapter 3 — sloth
Chapter 7 — anteater	Chapter 16 — howler monkey
Chapter 20 — terrapin	Chapter 20 — harpy eagle
Chapter 21 — anaconda	Chapter 23 — macaw

Illustration © 2010, Karen Donnelly.

SCHOLASTIC
www.scholastic.co.uk

READ & RESPOND: Activities based on *Journey to the River Sea*

Assessment

Assessment advice

Journey to the River Sea is a historical novel that presents all the confrontations and drama of a great dilemma story. As such, one effective focus for assessment is to look at the children's understanding of the points of view of the various characters. Can they see the different motives at play within the characters? Can they express their views regarding the way these various perspectives react to each other?

The activity below provides a way of opening out characterisation and exploring how these characters react to each other.

As the children undertake this activity, look out for the way they pick up on the themes of the story. The characters take different stances between freedom and restriction, and Maia, Clovis and Miss Minton change over time. The twins and Finn remain fairly constant – though all are affected by the encounters they experience in the story.

The focus of assessment here should be the children's ability to express the different points of view the characters take and then to see how these link to the themes of the story as a whole.

Character clicks

> **Assessment focus:** To understand underlying themes, causes and points of view.
> **What you need:** Copies of *Journey to the River Sea*, photocopiable page 32, scissors and exercise books.
> **Cross-curricular link:** PSHE.

What to do

● Point out the fact that *Journey to the River Sea* is a novel filled with different characters who meet and interact with each other. Working with the whole class, list some of the characters the children can recall from the story. An exhaustive list would be extensive and challenging.

● Working in groups, ask the children to cut out the character cards provided on photocopiable page 32, shuffle them and place them face down on the table.

● Invite each child to take two cards at random and see what pairing they end up with. Encourage them to imagine what each of these characters would think of the other – either through what we know from the text directly or though inferring from how these characters have behaved in the story described in *Journey to the River Sea*. (For less confident learners, limit the character cards to those relating to Finn, Maia, the twins and Miss Minton, and select some clear examples.)

● Ask the children to repeat the task a few times and, whenever they come to an interesting pairing, to jot down some notes in their book, recording the way they think these two characters respond to each other.

● Once the children have completed this task, end with a whole-class session, sharing some of the more interesting connections.

Character clicks

Maia	Miss Minton

Clovis	**Finn**

Beatrice/Gwendolyn	**Mrs Carter**

The Professor	**The crows**
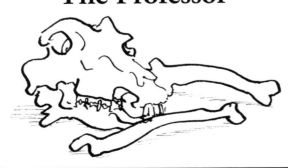	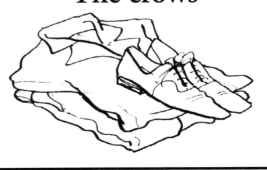

SCHOLASTIC
www.scholastic.co.uk

Illustration © 2010, Karen Donnelly.